PAOLA NAVONE
EDITED BY CAROLINE KLEIN

Straightforward, instinctive, eclectic and a dreamer. In her vision, forms from the West blend with flavors and colors from the East and from the southern parts of the world that she knows and loves deeply. Captivated by these cultures, they are at the root of her untiring passion for the history of handicrafts, for artisan techniques, for the material culture of places both near and faraway. Free-spirited, curious, cosmopolitan, traveler of the world. An atypical nomad who likes to put down roots anywhere and everywhere she sets up home, no matter if it is for a lifetime or just a short holiday. Traveling and living abroad has nourished her special ability to look at, or better yet, to see everything around her. The details and the anomalies. The archetypes and the differences. A gift, cultivated every day that represents her way of breathing. In her intuitive world, stylistic consistencies are not nurtured. On the contrary, she loves to work with diverse things, looking in many different directions in order to discover new relationships and to assemble all these things that exist in the world in an ironic way. It is not always necessary to venture far: memories and familiar passages often hide enticing wonders. When asked to talk about her work, she loves to describe how every single project is the fruit of an encounter with special people, how this alchemy, which is different each time, is her true impetus toward creativity. An enchantment that is able to lead down long, unexpected and creative paths. More than a designer, Paola Navone is an anthropologist of things, studying the history, shape and substance of artifacts that come from diverse cultures and times, in order to uncover their secrets and experiment with new associations of taste. Because ideas are capable of circulating by means of objects and they are able to go anywhere. Of course, we are dealing with the here-and-now but it is a contemporaneity that loves to contaminate its own useless purity with the energy and beauty of the world. All of Paola Navone's projects talk – in the anti-theoretical and anarchic sentimental way that distinguishes her – about that rich, vital and open relationship with the world.

Aufrichtig, instinktiv, eklektisch und voller Träume. In ihrer Vorstellung vermischen sich westliche Formen mit den Düften und Farben des Orients und des Weltsüdens, die sie gut kennt und liebt. Von diesen Kulturen verzaubert, hegt sie eine unermüdliche Leidenschaft für die Geschichte der Manufakturen, für Handwerkstechniken, sowie für die Materialkultur nah und weit entfernter Orte. Eine freiheitsliebende, neugierige, kosmopolitische Weltreisende; eine atypische Nomadin, die überall dort, wo sie für sich selbst Häuser einrichtet, Wurzeln schlägt, unabhängig davon, ob es für ein Leben oder nur einen kurzen Ferienaufenthalt ist. Die Reisen und das Leben in fremden Ländern haben ihre besondere Fähigkeit, Dinge zu betrachten und all das, was sie umgibt, zu sehen, zu entdecken, gefördert: Die Details und die Anomalien, die Archetypen und die Unterschiede. Eine Gabe, die sie Tag für Tag sorgfältig pflegt und für sie eine Form des Atmens bedeutet. Ihre Intuitionen folgen keinen stilistischen Regeln: Ganz im Gegenteil liebt sie es, mit unterschiedlichen Dingen zu arbeiten und in verschiedene Richtungen zu schauen, um neue Beziehungen aufzutun und das, was in der Welt existiert, auf ironische Weise miteinander zu verbinden. Es ist nicht immer notwendig, in die Ferne zu schweifen! Erinnerungen und vertraute Wege verbergen häufig Wunder. Befragt man sie zu ihrer Arbeit, liebt sie es, darüber zu berichten, wie jedes einzelne Projekt Frucht einer speziellen Begegnung ist. Und dass diese, immer andersartige Alchimie, den wahren Kreativitätsimpuls darstellt und unerwartete Wege eröffnet. Paola Navone ist eher Anthropologin von Gegenständen als Designerin. Sie studiert die Geschichte, die Form und die Substanz von Kunsthandwerk verschiedener Kulturen und Zeiten, um Geheimnisse aufzudecken und mit neuartigen Geschmackverbindungen zu experimentieren. Ideen kreisen in allen Gegenständen und können überall ankommen. Natürlich im Hier und Jetzt. Jedoch in einer Gegenwart, die es liebt, ihre eigene, nutzlose Reinheit mit der Energie und Schönheit der Welt zu verunreinigen. Ihre Entwürfe erzählen auf antitheoretische und anarchisch-sentimentale Weise von ihrer reichen, lebenswichtigen und freien Beziehung zur Welt.

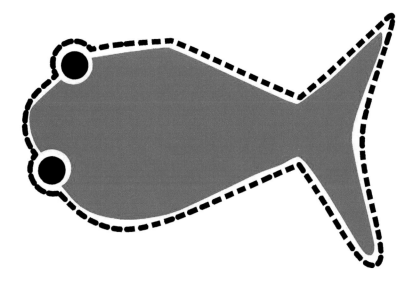

Abierta, instintiva, ecléctica y soñadora. En sus visiones las formas de Occidente se funden con sabores y colores de Oriente y del sur del mundo, que ella conoce y ama profundamente. De la fascinación por estos mundos nace su pasión por la historia de las manufacturas, por las técnicas artesanales, por la cultura material de sitios cercanos y lejanos. Libre, curiosa, cosmopolita, grande viajera. Una nómada atípica que adora echar raíces en cualquier sitio en el que viva, por la vida o por una breve vacación, no es importante. Viajando y viviendo en muchos sitios ha nutrido su especial capacidad de mirar, o mejor dicho de ver, lo que está a su alrededor. Los detalles y las anomalías. Los arquetipos y las diferencias. Un don cultivado día a día que es como su modo de respirar. En su mundo de intuiciones no cultiva la coherencia estilística. Le parece maravilloso trabajar con la diversidad y mirar en muchas direcciones para encontrar nuevas relaciones entre las cosas y coordinar irónicamente lo que ve en el mundo. No siempre es necesario ir lejos: memorias y paisajes familiares a menudo esconden maravillas. Cuando le piden que hable de su trabajo, dice que sus proyectos nacen de encuentros con personas especiales. Que esa alquimia, diferente en cada caso, para ella es el verdadero impulso hacia la creatividad. Un encantamiento capaz de enhebrar prolongados e inesperados itinerarios creativos. Más que una diseñadora Paola Navone es una antropóloga de las cosas que estudia la historia, la forma y la sustancia de manufacturas nacidas en tiempos y lugares diferentes para comprender sus secretos y experimentar nuevas comuniones de gusto. Porque las ideas circulan a través de los objetos y pueden llegar a cualquier lugar. Viviendo la contemporaneidad, por cierto, pero esa que desea contaminar su inútil pureza con la energía y la belleza del mundo. Cada una de sus acciones creativas cuenta – en el modo antiteórico y anárquico sentimental que la distingue – de su rica, vital y libre relación con el mundo.

Instinctive, éclectique, productive et visionnaire. Paola Navone se nourrit de différents univers, mêle avec passion, formes et couleurs, Occident et Orient et saveurs rapportées d'un Sud qu'elle aime profondément. Fascinée par ces autres mondes, elle s'est attachée à la culture matérielle des lieux proches et lointains, s'est initiée aux artisanats et à leurs techniques, aux objets et à leurs histoires. Libre, curieuse, cosmopolite, grande voyageuse, cette nomade atypique s'enracine partout où elle s'installe, que ce soit pour la vie ou le temps d'une parenthèse. C'est en voyageant et en vivant à l'étranger qu'elle a développé un talent, une façon très personnelle de regarder, d'interpréter ce qui l'entoure. Les détails et les anomalies. Les archétypes et les différences. Ce monde d'intuitions ne s'embarrasse pas de cohérences stylistiques. Elle y travaille les diversités en suivant tous les champs d'investigation qui s'offrent à elle. Navone a le chic pour redécouvrir des formes anciennes qu'elle réveille avec aplomb. Elle absorbe les traditions et les remodèle, assemble des éléments apparemment inconciliables. Histoire d'imaginer de nouvelles relations entre les choses qui existent dans son monde ou de leur réinventer avec humour de nouvelles vies. Est-il d'ailleurs nécessaire d'aller chercher bien loin ? Mémoires et lieux familiers dissimulent souvent des merveilles reconnaît celle qui explique son travail en racontant que chacun de ses projets est le fruit d'une rencontre, d'un échange. Et que c'est cette alchimie des personnalités, à chaque fois unique, qui provoque le véritable élan créatif et les parcours parfois inattendus. Designer mais aussi anthropologue des choses, Navone étudie l'histoire, la forme et la substance d'objets créés à des époques anciennes et dans des lieux multiples, pour mieux deviner leurs secrets et activer des complicités de goût inédites. Elle sait que les idées circulent à travers les objets et peuvent surgir de n'importe où. Que la pureté inutile se doit être bouleversée par l'énergie et la beauté contemporaines de notre univers. Chaque geste de ses projets traduit – dans le style anarchique et sentimental qui la caractérise – sa relation au monde, riche, vitale et libre

Schietta, istintiva, eclettica e sognatrice. Nelle sue visioni le forme dell'Occidente si fondono a sapori e colori portati dall'Oriente e dal sud del mondo che lei conosce e ama profondamente. Dall'incanto per questi mondi nasce la sua passione per la storia dei manufatti, per le tecniche artigiane, per la cultura materiale di luoghi vicini e lontani. Libera, curiosa, cosmopolita, grande viaggiatrice. Una nomade atipica che ama mettere radici dovunque prenda casa, se per la vita o per una breve vacanza, non è importante. Viaggiando e vivendo altrove ha alimentato la sua speciale attitudine a guardare, o meglio a vedere, ciò che le sta intorno. I dettagli e le anomalie. Gli archetipi e le differenze. Un dono coltivato ogni giorno che rappresenta il suo modo di respirare. Nel suo mondo di intuizioni non coltiva la coerenza stilistica. Trova invece meraviglioso lavorare con le diversità e guardare in molte direzioni per trovare nuove relazioni tra le cose e mettere insieme in modo ironico ciò che esiste nel mondo. Non sempre serve andare lontano: memorie e passaggi familiari nascondono spesso meraviglie. Quando le chiedono di parlare del suo lavoro, ama raccontare come ogni suo progetto nasca da un incontro con persone speciali. Come questa alchimia, ogni volta diversa, sia per lei la vera spinta alla creatività. Un incanto capace di condurre lunghi percorsi creativi inaspettati. Più che una designer Paola Navone è un'antropologa delle cose che studia la storia, la forma e la sostanza di manufatti nati in tempi e luoghi diversi per comprenderne i segreti e sperimentare nuove comunanze di gusto. Perché le idee circolano attraverso gli oggetti e possono arrivare ovunque. Vivendo la contemporaneità certo, ma quella che ami contaminare la propria inutile purezza con l'energia e la bellezza del mondo. Ogni suo gesto progettuale racconta – nel modo anti-teorico e anarchico sentimentale che la distingue – di questa sua ricca, vitale e libera relazione con il mondo.

INTERIORS

Paola Navone creates domestic landscapes able to reassure, excite and surprise every time, thanks to some amusing touch. The ruse might consist of the use of everyday objects placed out of context, or by multiplying something banal to the point that it becomes extraordinary. Houses and exhibit designs are based on the contamination between contrasts: light and dark colors, precious and inexpensive materials, rare and common objects. The rule is to experiment, to trespass the boundaries, to mix with irony. To surprise through modern, poetic associations and improbable combinations. To provoke a childlike curiosity that moves us to rummage beyond what is easily in sight. On one hand the passion for tradition, archetypes and things that endure, unchanged over time. On the other, the inebriation of the ephemeral, of temporary set ups that Paola Navone loves to interpret as if they were amazing cabinets of curiosities, magical places that speak about the world through objects.

Paola Navone erzeugt Wohnlandschaften, die beruhigen, erregen und dank ihres amüsanten Charakters stets überraschen. Mit Geschick versetzt sie Alltagsgegenstände aus ihrem gewohnten Kontext, oder vervielfältigt Banales, bis es etwas Besonderes wird. Häuser und Ausstellungen beruhen auf Gegensätzen, die sich gegenseitig kontaminieren: Helle und dunkle Farben, kostbares und einfaches Material, seltene und gewöhnliche Gegenstände. Es gilt, zu experimentieren, die Grenzen zu überschreiten, mit Ironie zu vermischen und durch moderne, poetische Assoziationen und unwahrscheinliche Kombinationen zu überraschen. Die kindliche Neugier hervorzurufen, sowie durch die zum Durchstöbern und Erkunden einlädt. Einerseits die Leidenschaft für Traditionen, Archetypen und Dinge, die unverändert bleiben. Andererseits die Begeisterung für das Kurzweilige, für temporäre Installationen, die Paola Navone mit Vorliebe als sagenhafte Wunderkammern interpretiert, als magische Orte, in denen Gegenstände von der Welt erzählen.

Paola Navone crea paisajes domésticos que tranquilizan, emocionan y maravillan siempre por un toque divertido. El artificio puede consistir en usar cosas cotidianas fuera de su contexto. O multiplicar lo banal hasta convertirlo en extraordinario. Casas e instalaciones están construidos con la contaminación entre contrastes: colores claros y colores oscuros, materiales preciosos y materiales pobres, objetos raros y objetos comunes. La regla es experimentar, superar fronteras e hibridar con ironía. Sorprender con asociaciones modernas, poéticas wy combinaciones imprevistas. Suscitar esa curiosidad infantil que hace hurgar más allá de lo que se ve. Por un lado la pasión por las tradiciones, los arquetipos y las cosas que se mantienen inmutables. Por el otro, la ebriedad de lo efímero, la pasión por los montajes temporales, que Paola Navone sabe concebir como asombrosas cámaras de las maravillas, lugares mágicos que hablan del mundo a través de los objetos.

Paola Navone crée des paysages domestiques qui rassurent, émeuvent ou étonnent. Quitte à joyeusement détourner des objets quotidiens de leur contexte ou de multiplier le banal pour le rendre extraordinaire. Maisons et installations sont bâties sur la mise en scène et la contamination des contrastes. Elle y fait cohabiter couleurs claires et couleurs sombres, matériaux bruts et raffinés, élèments rares et objets quotidiens. La règle est d'expérimenter, de bousculer les limites et d'assembler avec allégresse. De surprendre grâce à des rapprochements modernes, poétiques, à des associations improbables. Ou bien encore de susciter la curiosité enfantine qui va fouiller au-delà des apparences. A sa passion des traditions, des archétypes et de ce qui dure, répond son ivresse de l'éphémère, la nécessité originelle du temporaire. Paola Navone déroule et interprète les espaces comme de mirobolantes chambres des merveilles, des lieux magiques qui revèlent le monde.

Paola Navone crea paesaggi domestici capaci di rassicurare, emozionare e meravigliare ogni volta per un accento divertito. L'artificio può essere quello di usare cose di tutti i giorni fuori dal loro contesto. O di moltiplicare il banale fino a renderlo straordinario. Case e allestimenti sono costruiti sulla contaminazione tra cose contrastanti: colori chiari e colori scuri, materiali preziosi e materiali poveri, oggetti rari e oggetti comuni. La regola è sperimentare, sconfinare e ibridare con ironia. Sorprendere attraverso accostamenti moderni e poetici e associazioni improbabili. Suscitare quella curiosità infantile che muove a frugare oltre a ciò che si vede. Da una parte la passione per le tradizioni, gli archetipi e le cose che durano immutate nel tempo. Dall'altra l'ebbrezza per l'effimero, la passione per gli allestimenti temporanei, che Paola Navone ama interpretare come mirabolanti camere delle meraviglie, luoghi magici che parlano del mondo attraverso gli oggetti.

RESIDENCE
Milan, Italy | 1995

RESIDENCE
Paris, France | 2007

MONDO
Installation
Milan, Italy | 1993

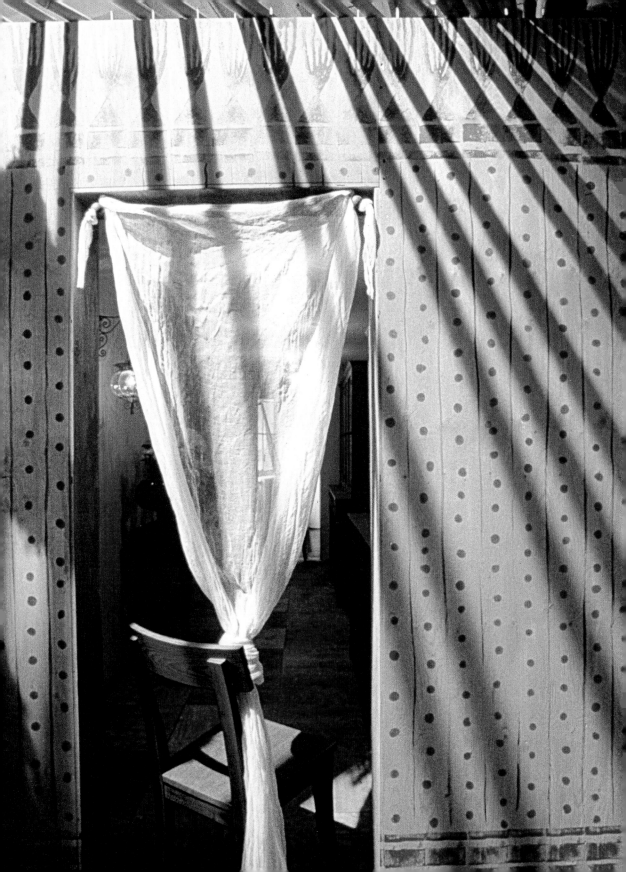

PER FILO E PER SEGNO
Exhibition
Organizer: Fondazione per il libro,
la musica e la cultura
Turin, Italy | 2003

NO WALLS
Installation
Client: Spotti Shop
Milan, Italy | 2009

RICHARD GINORI @ TAST

• GOOD FOOD • GOOD RELAX • GOOD MAG

CONCEPT
PAOLA NAVONE

SET UP
OTTO design - Runz Ricciardelli Davide Lodde

STYLE
OTTO design - François Bernard, Douglas Legg
Cristina Pettenuzzo, Carolina Buonocore

PHOTOGRAPHY
Enrico Conti

LOUNGE FURNITURE
BAXTER www.baxter.it

PRODUCTION
Scenart, Angelo Grassi & C.

LIGHTING
Flli Edison

MAGS
Happy Books

FOOD & WINE RESEARCH
Davide Paolini

FOOD DESIGN PROJECT
Arabeschi di Latte

CATERING
Galateo Ricevimenti Firenze - Milano

for TASTE
Antonio Mattei - Desoc
Cearnochi Luccheschi Az. Agr.
Da Re - I Bitacuci
Dal Bello Az. Agr.
Donnarugata
Friulrosa
Ghezzi - Sangiolaro
Giordano 1936
Luigi Guffanti Fiori formaggi 1876
Osteria de L'ortolano
Prosciuttificio Dok dall'Ava
Salumificio MEC Palmieri

ACQUA - Galvanina

for RICHARD GINORI 1735
Alberto Pianteni Giampaolo Piazzini, Stefano Guidotti
Valentina Puggelli, Luca Schwarz, Elena Serrotti
Paolo Pratellesi, Marcello Bongini, Tersillo Fabri
Piero Luchi, Stefano Forsti, Lorenzo Magnolfi
Stefano Puggelli, Vincenzo Rizzo
Martina Chniola, Laura Ceriotti

for PITTI IMMAGINE
Rachele Saltini, Alessandro Buompadre,
Francesca Disterno, Manuela Gazzaniga,
Francesca Lonzi, Roberto Ruta

10

RICHARD GINORI @ TASTE LOUNGE
Installation
For Richard Ginori + Pitti Immagine
Milan, Italy | 2009

GLASS JEWELRY SHOP
Shop Design
Client: Salviati
Paris, France | 2005

PANE E ACQUA
Restaurant Design
Client: Rossana Orlandi Gallery
Milan, Italy | 2008 – 2009

PRODUCTS

"People do not care about knowing what an armchair represents. They simply want a comfortable armchair with warmth and character." With this conviction Paola Navone creates objects customized for the body and soul, things of simple poetry with natural expressiveness. She takes her inexhaustible inspiration from everything that surrounds her. Discovering forms and artefacts from distant traditions and reinterpreting them in a contemporary way is one of her special talents. Special, too, is her love for the tactile nature of things, for the feel of materials, for their practicality that – free from myths about methodology – expresses the magic of ancient handwork. Her objects are in the balance between design and handicraft. They come to be in unconventional ways, through subtle influences, an unexpected gesture, or even by way of happy accidents that can magically short-circuit the monotony of serial production. Friendly objects, with non-aggressive forms, created for adapting and adjusting themselves to the houses they happen upon, revealing, in this way, their uniqueness.

„Die Leute wollen nicht darüber nachdenken, was ein Sessel über ihre Persönlichkeit aussagt. Sie wollen einfach einen bequemen Sessel mit Wärme und Charakter haben." Aus dieser Überzeugung erschafft Paola Navone Möbel, maßgeschneidert auf Leib und Seele, Dinge von schlichter Poesie und natürlichem Ausdruck. Sie schöpft aus allem, was sie umgibt, Inspiration. Formen und Manufakturen aus entfernten Traditionen zu entdecken und diese auf zeitgenössische Weise zu interpretieren, ist eines ihrer besonderen Talente. So besonders wie auch ihre Liebe für die taktilen Eigenschaften von Material, für das Nützliche, das – frei vom Mythos der Methode – die Magie alter Handarbeit ausdrückt. Ihre Gegenstände sind in der Schwebe zwischen Design und Handfertigkeit und können auf unkonventionelle Art entstehen: durch Einflüsse, unerwartete Gesten, oder sogar durch Unfälle bei der Herstellung, die die Monotonie der Serienproduktion auf wundersame Weise brechen können. Freundliche Objekte nicht aggressiver Gestalt, die dazu erdacht sind, sich den Häusern, auf die sie treffen, anzupassen, sich zu verändern und somit ihre Einzigartigkeit zu offenbaren.

"La gente no quiere saber lo que representa un sillón. Sencillamente, quiere un sillón cómodo, cálido y envolvente". Partiendo de esta idea Paola Navone diseña objetos a la medida del cuerpo y del alma. Cosas de sencilla poesía y de natural expresividad. Lo que la rodea es una fuente inagotable de inspiración. Descubrir formas y objetos de tradiciones lejanas e interpretarlos en clave contemporánea es su talento especial. Así como especial es su amor por lo táctil, por la captación de la materia, por la practicidad que – libre del mito del método – expresa la magia de manualidades antiguas. Sus objetos están en equilibrio entre diseño y artesanía. Pueden nacer de una manera absolutamente no convencional, de una sugestión, de un gesto insólito o de un incidente casual capaz de romper mágicamente la monotonía de lo serial. Objetos *friendly* con formas no agresivas, pensados para adaptarse y transformarse en las casas que encuentran. Y develar de este modo su unicidad.

« Les gens ne veulent pas savoir ce qu'un fauteuil représente. Ils veulent simplement un fauteuil confortable, chaud et enveloppant. » Partant de ce principe, Paola Navone dessine des objets faits sur mesure pour le corps et pour l'âme. Des élèments qui expriment naturellement poésie et simplicité. Ce qui l'entoure reste une source d'inspiration inépuisable. Elle accumule et collectionne. Elle chine dans le monde entier, traque l'objet inhabituel, le fait main, la pièce unique qu'elle ne veut pas laisser tomber dans l'oubli. Elle a ce don particulier de mixer esprit industriel et surprise artistique, de fondre styles et techniques, de brouiller traditions et innovations. De toujours reinterprètrer dans la juste perspective. Contemporaine. Elle revendique la sensualité et le goût des matières, s'approprie le savoir-faire des methods ancestrales. Ses objets à mi-chemin entre design et artisanat, peuvent naitre d'une suggestion, d'un geste inhabituel ou d'un incident de parcours qui va briser la monotonie de la fabrication en série. Un design qu'elle ne veut pas agressif, conçu pour s'adapter et se transformer au grè des maisons qu'il rencontre. Et ainsi se révèler. Unique

"La gente non vuole sapere cosa una poltrona rappresenta. Vuole semplicemente una poltrona comoda, calda e avvolgente". Partendo da questa idea Paola Navone disegna oggetti fatti su misura per il corpo e per l'anima. Cose di semplice poesia e di naturale espressività. Ciò che le sta intorno è per lei un'inesauribile fonte di ispirazione. Scoprire forme e manufatti di tradizioni lontane e interpretarli in chiave contemporanea è un suo talento speciale. Come speciale è il suo amore per la tattilità, per il senso della materia, per la praticità che – libera dal mito del metodo – esprime la magia di manualità antiche. I suoi oggetti sono in bilico tra design e artigianato. Possono nascere in modo non convenzionale, da una suggestione, da un gesto inaspettato o da un incidente di percorso capace di rompere magicamente la monotonia della serialità. Oggetti *friendly* dalla forma non aggressiva, pensati per adattarsi e trasformarsi nelle case che incontrano. E svelare in questo modo la loro unicità.

BAXTER
Punto Rosso, Punto Oro, Black & White
2005 – 2008

DRIADE
The white snow, Paloma
1999

EGIZIA
Chandi, Alibaba | 2004 – 2006

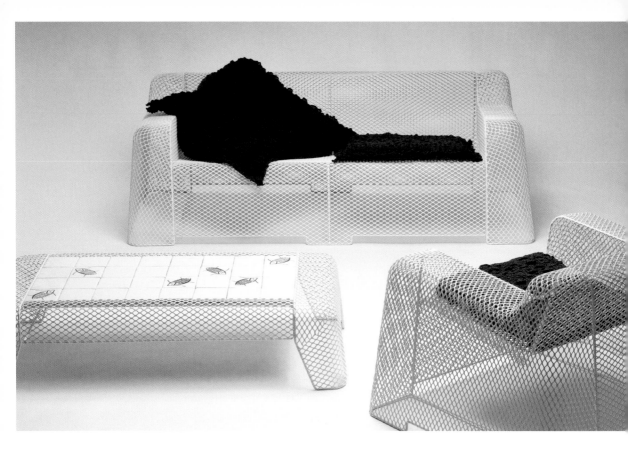

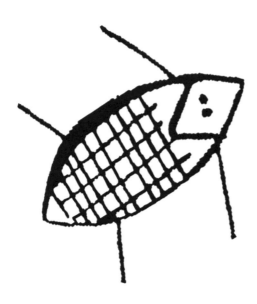

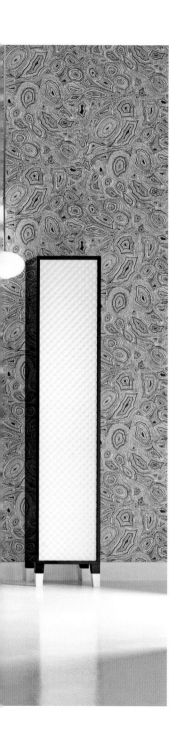

FALPER
Coco, Menhir, Peace Hotel | 2008

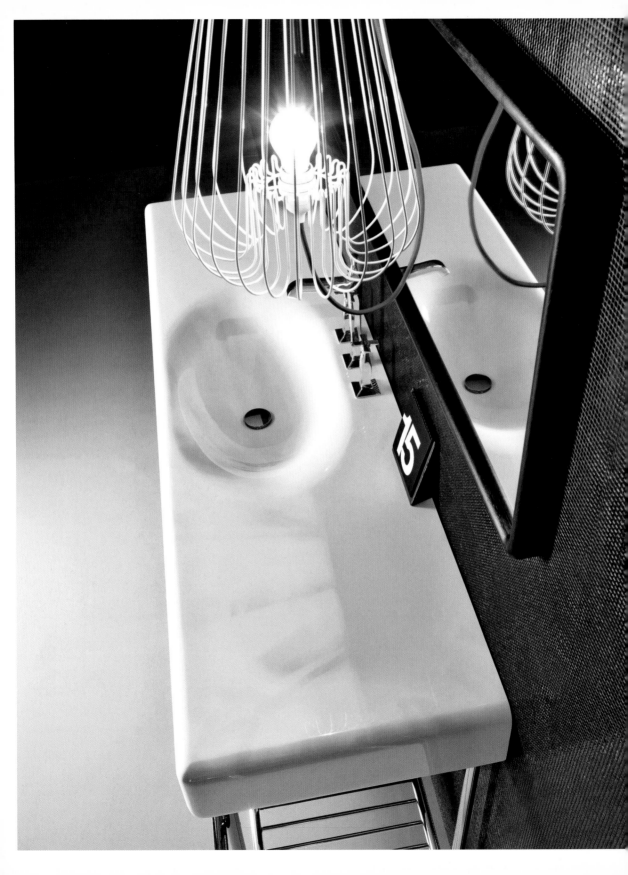

GERVASONI
Allu, Blue, Ghost, Gray, In Out, Slim, Sweet, Tiger
2002 – 2009

RICHARD GINORI
Broken, Sesonrosefioriranno, Provaprima, Blueprint
2009

HABITAT
Mara, Lapulapu | 2009

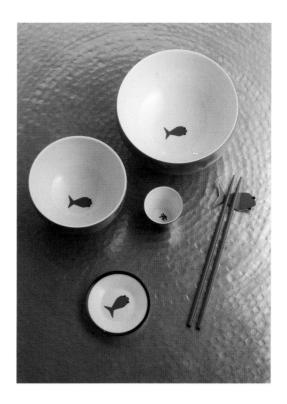

LANDO
Gingerbread | 2005 – 2008

MAMOLI
Paola&TheKitchen | 2010

IVANO REDAELLI
Striptease | 2008

REICHENBACH
Taste, New Baroque Silver Shiny Glaze, Blue Taste, Flower
2005 – 2010

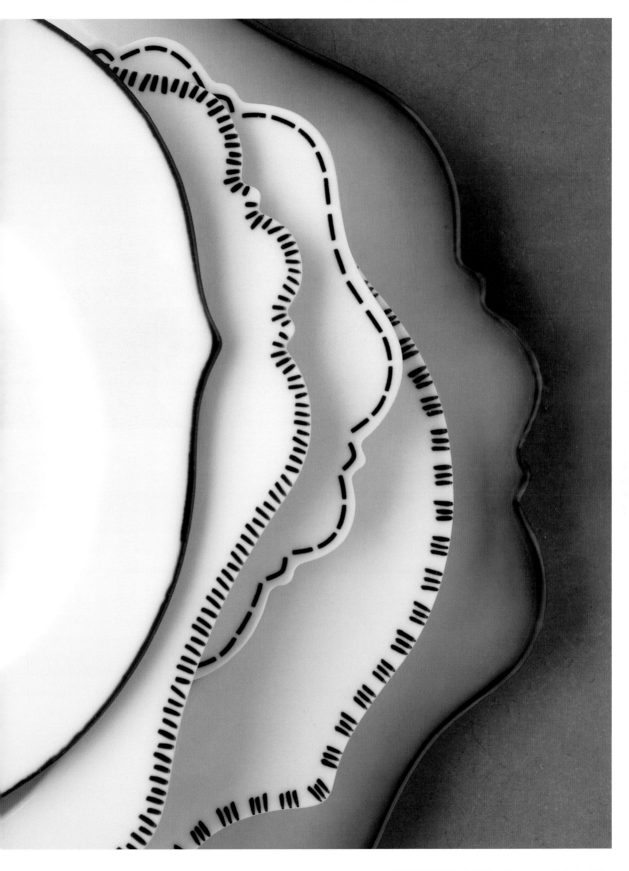

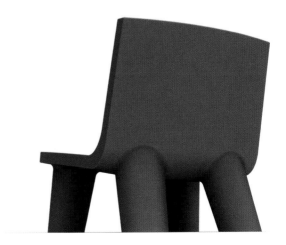

SLIDE
Low Lita | 2008

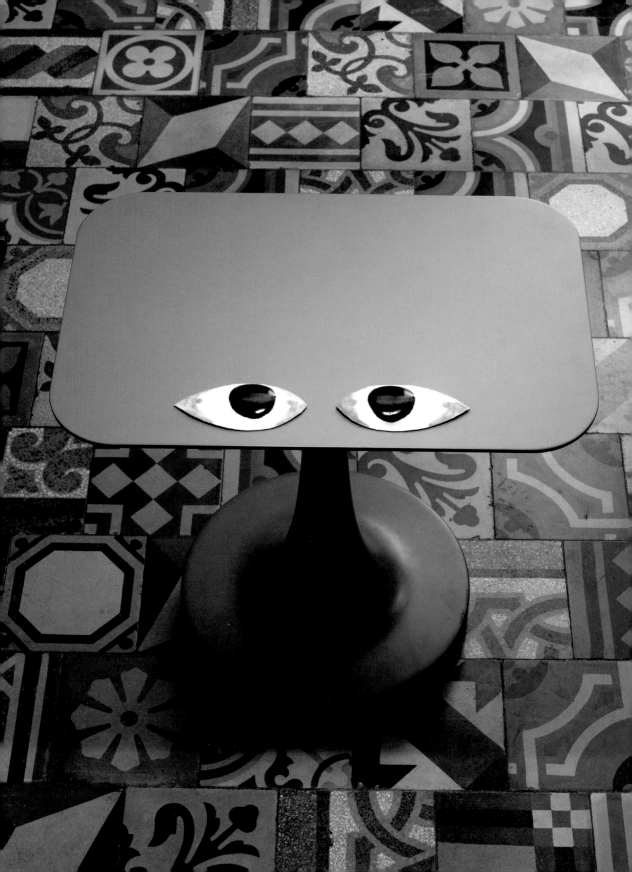

ONE OFF PROJECTS

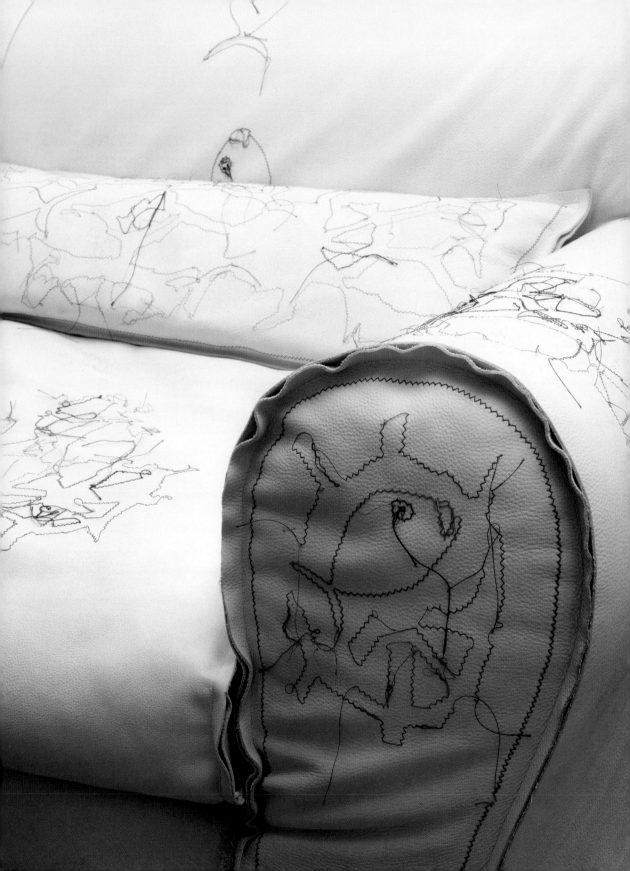

INDEX

PAOLA NAVONE
Corso San Gottardo, 22
20136 Milano, Italy
Tel. +39 02 58104926
Fax +39 02 58112397
info@paolanavone.it
www.paolanavone.it

Paola Navone

Born in Turin, lives and works in Milan and Paris although she is first and foremost a citizen of the world.

During her studies Paola Navone went to Florence, because of her attraction towards the anti-academic and radical architecture groups Archizoom, Superstudio and Ufo that worked on visionary, brave projects and rejected the traditional concept of design. The reasons of the cultured debate that she absorbed during her formation intertwined without antagonism with her global character. Right after her graduation in architecture, she went to Cameroon together with an ethnologist in order to study an ex-nomadic people for whom she drew houses. Between 1970 and 1980, she worked in Milan alongside Alessandro Mendini, Ettore Sottsass and Andrea Branzi who, coordinated by Alessandro Guerriero, founded the Alchimia group, the most progressive set on the Italian design scene, developing a highly productive and stimulating avant-garde stance. Many instances of that world became strong references: the emotion beyond the function, the social value of the expressive creativity, the ethical function of the industry, the value of the surface compared to the structure. Between 1984 and 2000 she lived in different Asian countries where she discovered new cultures able to create unusual and unexpected things. In the Far East it is possible to realize ideas and projects that you would never be able to achieve in the Milanese office. This experience consolidates her natural propensity to the contamination between things. In her long and many-sided career she has switched and she still switches easily between the roles of architect, designer, art director, interior decorator, set designer, critic as well as organizer of exhibitions and events. She designs interiors for homes, restaurants, showrooms, offices, shops and concepts for many important exhibitions across the world.

Team

Carlo Ballabio, Carolina Buonocore, Gloria Castro, Valentina Ghiringhelli, Ornella Gioé, Ernesto Iadevaia, Davide Loddo, Cristina Pettenuzzo, Cecilia Proserpio, Rune Ricciarelli, Lucia Rosatone, Anna Sara Zanolla Mancini

Clients

Abet Laminati, Alcantara, Alessi, Antonangeli, Arcade, Bab Anmil, Baxter, Bisazza, Bontempi, Casamilano, Ceramica Viva, Ciatti, Dada, Driade, Egizia, Emu, Eno, Facebox, Falper, Gervasoni, Richard Ginori, Habitat, Idealform, Italamp, Illy, Knoll International, Lando, Mamoli, Molteni, Mondo, Natuzzi, Oltrefrontiera, Orizzonti, Poliform, Pomellato, Piazza Sempione, Ivano Redaelli, Reichenbach, Riva 1920, Roche Bobois, Slide, Swarovski, Terreblu

Exhibit Design

1975/79 "Gli anni 50" exhibition market of Naj Oleari, CentroKappa Kartell, Noviglio, Milano

"La sedia di materiale plastico"

"Identità per gli artificiali" at Triennale di Milano, Italy

1980 "L'oggetto banale" - in collaboration with Alessandro Mendini, Daniela Puppa, Franco Raggi at Biennale of Venice, Italy

1983 "Mangiare con gli occhi" with Kazuko Sato at Centrodomus Milano, Italy

1985 "Cibo e piante", Manila, Philippines

1996 "Les îsles Philippines" at Printemps department store, Paris, France

1997 "Soft touch" at Ambiente, Frankfurt, Germany

"Italia in Cina" for Federtextile, Bejing, China

1999 "Le misure della convivialità" and "By name" at Pitti Immagine Casa, Florence, Italy

2000 "Nort-South-East-West" and "Nuove trame" at Pitti Immagine Casa, Florence, Italy

"Designer of the year" for A&W magazine, Cologne, Germany

2001 "Remix" at Ambiente, Frankfurt, Germany

"Ritratti d'autore" at Pitti Immagine Casa, Florence, Italy

2002 "Per filo e per segno" at Palazzo Carignano, Turin, Italy

2003 "Digital Print: una nuova generazione di superfici" at Triennale di Milano, Italy

2004 "Pitti Immagine Casa" exhibition concept at Fortezza del Basso, Florence, Italy

"Hard & Soft" at Abitare il Tempo, Verona, Italy

2005 "Villéage" exhibition concept at Salon Du Meuble, Paris, France

"Waterbar" at Ambiente, Frankfurt, Germany

"Heimtextil" exhibition concept, Frankfurt, Germany

"Textures & Materials" at Studiopiù, Milan, Italy

"Visioni a-moderne" at Triennale di Milano, Italy

"Doppio Gioco" at Abitare il Tempo, Verona, Italy

2006 Abitare il Tempo party concept at Giardini di Villa Giusti, Verona, Italy

2007 "Dream House" at Salon Futur Interieur, Paris, France

2008 "Non solo alimentari" at Pitti Taste, Florence, Italy

"Bianco 411" at Triennale di Milano, Italy

"Striptease" at Abitare il Tempo, Verona, Italy

2009 "Bar a Chocolat" + "Scène D'Intérieur" for Maison & Objet Editeurs, Paris, France

"Richard Ginori @ Taste Lounge" at Padiglione Visconti, Milan, Italy

2010 "Café des éditeurs" + "Salon de thé Mariage Frères" + "Noura Restaurant" for Maison & Objet Editeurs, Paris, France

Awards

1983 International Design Award, Osaka, Japan

1999 Prix d'éxcellence by Marie Claire Maison magazine, Paris, France

Prix createur de l'année by Maison et Object, Paris, France

2000 Designer of the year, by A&W magazine, Cologne, Germany

Photocredits

Enrico Conti

Andrea Ferrari

Eric Flogny/Aleph

Alessandro Paderni

Foto Maurizio Marcato

Alberto Mascheroni

Cristina Pettenuzzo

Laila Pozzo

Marta Zappalà

© 2013 DAAB MEDIA GMBH
   2nd Edition

Published and distributed worldwide by
DAAB MEDIA GMBH
Scheidtweilerstr. 69
50933 Cologne / Germany
tel. + 49 221 690 48 210
fax + 49 221 690 48 229
www.daab-media.com

Join our community
www.edaab.com
and present your work to a worldwide audience

Printed in Italy
www.graficheflaminia.com

ISBN 978-3-942597-02-9

Edited by Caroline Klein

Caroline Klein studied Interior Design in Florence and
Architecture at the Technical University of Munich. She
has been working for different renowned architectural
offices as well as a freelance writer, producer and editor
for international architectural magazines and publishers.

Concept by Ralf Daab
Creative director: Feyyaz
Layout by Sonia Mion, Nicola Iannibello
www.ventizeronove.it

Introductions by Caroline Klein

English translation by Caroline Klein, Mike Ryan
French translation by scriptum srl
German translation by Caroline Klein
Spanish translation by scriptum srl

Copy editing by Caroline Klein

Litho fgv GROUP, Milan
www.fgvgrafica.it